This notebook
belongs to

_____

Funny Office Notebooks
for smart people like you

Check out our other fun notebooks that you can use yourself or give out as gifts. And don't forget to leave a quick review.

Bored at Work • Snarky Office • Tired of Working
Corporate Ladder Guides • Executive Career Guides

The average raise is 3% but the average salary increase after switching jobs is 10-20%. Staying with the same company means earning 50% less over your lifetime than those who are strategically changing jobs.

24% of commuters say that when they are stuck in traffic, they think "deep" thoughts. What do you think about?

70% of Americans with full-time jobs are not inspired
by their work or their managers. That makes them
less productive and engaged at work.

King of France Louis XV was the first to use a stapler to bind his royal papers. Each staple had the insignia of the royal court and was made out of solid gold and encrusted with precious stones.

An average worker spends more than a quarter of their day reading and answering emails. If you check emails only at set times in the day, you will increase your productivity.

People who work nights are almost twice as likely to
have an accident than those who work day shifts.

A ballpoint pen has enough ink to draw a line that's two miles long. A pencil has enough graphite to go for 35 miles! You'd need almost half a million pens and 6,825 pencils to draw a line to the Moon.

After Monday, Friday is the second most likely day to call in sick.
I wonder why? Otherwise, Fridays are usually the day
when the office is much more positive and social.

Reserved for Random Thoughts

People with a best friend at work are seven times more likely
to fully engage in their work.

For maximum productivity, it's necessary that your desk is organized.

The average worker in America receives 200 email, paper,
and phone messages per day.

In a phenomenon called "karoshi," a high number of Japanese workers drop dead at their work desks due to their 60 to 70-hour workweeks. Every year, over 10,000 Japanese suffer "karoshi."

For every 1,470 resumes received, an employer will hire
only one person.

The average workweek in the US is surprisingly only 34.5 hours.
But for the hardest working age range of 25-54, it is 40.3.

Charles Darwin invented the modern office chair. He added wheels to his own chair so that he could move around his office easier.

People who don't get involved in office politics are
more successful and efficient at work.

One percent of US employers allow their employees
to take naps during working hours.

The three most common jobs in America are
a salesperson, a cashier, and a fast-food worker.

The United States lags far behind other industrialized nations in family-oriented policies such as maternity leave, paid sick days, and breastfeeding support.

Studies show that increased humor at the office does not detract from productivity or the ability to complete tasks that require concentration.

66% of full-time workers in the US say they are heavy drinkers
(five or more drinks per sitting at least five days per month)
versus only 5% of part-time workers.

The average office chair with wheels travels about eight miles per year.

A British study has found that we are happiest on Saturday evening at 7:26 PM. They also concluded that our lowest point is at 7:20 AM on Monday. You could've guessed that, right?

If you work past 40 hours a week, your productivity decreases by 50%.

Reserved for Great Ideas

Employees who have more control over the layout and design
of their workspace are healthier and happier at work.

Before the Pregnancy Discrimination Act in 1978, American women could actually get fired from a job for being pregnant!

People are more productive on days when they exercise before work.

More than 16% of new hires quit within their first seven days on the job.
31% quit within the first six months.

A typical work desk is home to 400 times more bacteria than the average toilet seat. Yikes! Time to clean your desk?

Laughter can lower your heart rate, reduce your blood pressure, and boost the function of your blood vessels. It improves your blood flow which reduces your chances of cardiovascular diseases.

Once an item is filed away, there is a 98% chance
it will never be seen again. Uh-oh!

Having live plants in your work environment helps productivity.

One quarter of office workers report a productivity
decrease in the summertime.

Almost 40% of young professionals in the US are so unhappy with the lack of paid parental leave that they'd be willing to move to another country because of it.

Monday is the most common sick day except in Australia.
Their most common sick day is Tuesday. G'day!

Nine out of ten Millennials are expected to change jobs
every three years. This means that most of them will have
15-20 jobs in their lifetimes.

It's a myth that NASA spent a million dollars to develop the space pen.
The Fisher Pen Company did that on their own while creating it.
Before 1967, NASA simply used pencils in space.

Employees who work under managers who integrate humor into their interactions report experiencing greater work satisfaction.

You can revive an old permanent marker by soaking it in a bit of rubbing alcohol until the ink starts to leak. Then, put the cap on and let it dry for 15 minutes. For regular markers, use water instead.

When office temperatures are low (68F/20C), employees make 44% more errors and are less productive than when it's warmer (77F/25C).

Reserved for the Bucket List

Employees who sit near a window are more productive
and are less likely to take extra days off.

Women business owners employ 35% more people
than all the Fortune 500 companies combined.

Leonardo Da Vinci is credited with writing the first resume.

The average office worker spends up to 50 minutes every day looking for lost files and other misplaced items. That's four hours a week, or about 200 hours a year – over eight whole 24-hour days!

Tuesday is the most productive day of the week.

Americans now spend more than 100 hours a year commuting to work.

Your brain can slow down dramatically with a mere 2% drop
in your body water. Staying hydrated by drinking a sufficient amount
of water or healthy liquids can increase your daily productivity by 14%.

Would you take a pay cut for a more light-hearted work environment?
55% of workers would take less pay to have more fun at work.

Eighty percent of jobs are gained through networking.

More people walk or bike to work in Alaska than any other US state.

Nearly 80% of American workers are dissatisfied with their jobs.

Focused 90 minutes of work followed by a 20-minute break will make you much more productive. Also, look into "The Pomodoro Technique".

A professional typist's fingers travel 12.6 miles
during an average workday.

Laughter boosts your immune system by enhancing your antibodies and increasing your immune cell count. This helps reduce your chances of getting sick and missing out on work.

Listening to music while working actually helps people
get things done faster.

Staring at the green color can make you more creative and productive.

In 1965, executive pay in the US was 20 times higher than average worker pay. Today, executive pay is around 300 times the worker pay!

Multitasking at work can drop your IQ by 10 points!
That's the equivalent of losing one night's sleep or
twice the effect of smoking marijuana.

On average, US businesses spend $250,000 per year
to cover the costs associated with employee turnover.

Reserved for Doodling